THE VALUE OF PATIENCE

The Story of the Wright Brothers

VALUE COMMUNICATIONS, INC.
PUBLISHERS
LA JOLLA, CALIFORNIA

THE VALUE OF PATIENCE

The Story of the
Wright Brothers

BY SPENCER JOHNSON, M.D.

Second Edition
Manufactured in the United States of America
For information write to: Value Tales, P.O. Box 1012
La Jolla, CA 92038

Library of Congress Cataloging in Publication Data

Johnson, Spencer.
 The value of patience.

 First ed. published in 1975 under title: The ValueTale of the Wright Brothers.
 SUMMARY: Describes the patient efforts of the Wright Brothers to build a flying machine.
 1. Wright, Orville, 1871-1948—Juvenile literature.
2. Wright, Wilbur, 1867-1912—Juvenile
literature. 3. Aeronautics—United States—Biography—Juvenile literature. 4. Patience—Juvenile literature.
[1. Wright, Orville, 1871-1948. 2. Wright, Wilbur, 1867-1912. 3. Aeronautics—Biography. 4. Patience]
I. Pileggi, Steve. II. Title.
TL540.W7J62   629.13′092′2 [B] [920]   76-55022
ISBN 0-916392-08-2

Dedicated to
Tony, Stephany, and Barbara.

This tale is about two brothers who were patient.
The story that follows is based on events in their
lives. More historical facts about the Wright
Brothers can be found on page 61.

*O*nce upon a time...
there lived two brothers—Orville Wright and
Wilbur Wright.

One day the Wright Brothers were playing with their
friend Jimmy. They were building a toy cabin. They
liked to build things. And they were waiting for their
father to come home from a trip.

"Sometimes he brings us a present," said Wilbur.

"I hear him coming now," said Orville.

The front door opened, and in came the boys' father.

"He *did* bring you a present," said Jimmy. When he saw the odd little object in Mr. Wright's hand, he said, "But what a funny present!"

"What is it, Daddy?" asked the Wright Brothers.

"It's a new toy," said Mr. Wright. "When you throw it up in the air, it flies."

"It does?" said Wilbur. "Can we see it fly?" asked Orville. "Of course," said their father.

"It's a little bit like a bird," said Mr. Wright, and he threw the toy into the air.

It whirled up toward the ceiling.

It *was* a bit like a bird, but only a very little bit. When it hit the ceiling, what do you suppose happened?

That's right!

It came crashing down to the floor again.

The Wright Brothers felt very sad when they saw the toy fall.

''It flies, but not very well,'' said the boys' friend Jimmy.

Mr. Wright smiled. ''Throw it again,'' he said. ''Maybe it will stay up in the air a little longer.''

So the boys tossed the toy into the air again. This time it spun out across the room.

"It flies! It does fly!" shouted the boys.

"Golly!" said Jimmy.

To be sure, it was only a toy. But it gave the Wright Brothers a wonderful idea.

They were so happy that they started to dream. Do you know what they started to dream about?

"Suppose that toy was a *big* flying machine," thought the Wright Brothers.

"Suppose it could stay up in the air for a long time.

"We could climb aboard and steer it, and fly anywhere we wanted to go, right over the rooftops and trees!"

They knew it was only a dream. At that time people could float high in the air in balloons, or could fly for very short distances in gliders, but no one had ever made a real flying machine.

"No one will ever make a real flying machine," laughed the boys' friend Jimmy. "Look at that!"

And the little flying toy again fell to the floor.

"But that's only a toy," said Orville.

"If we made a *real* flying machine . . ." Wilbur began.

"You could never do it," said Jimmy. "You're silly, and I'm going to my own house and play with my own toys."

And he left.

The Wright Brothers might have been upset about this if they had had time. Before they could worry too much about Jimmy, however, they heard a strange, chirpy little voice talking to them.

The Wright Brothers looked around. They saw a bright-eyed bird perched on the windowsill. Then they pretended that the bird was talking to them.

"I wouldn't pay too much attention to your rude little friend," the bird said. "There really are some things that can stay up in the air for a long time. Take me, for instance. I fly much higher and much longer than any little whirly toy. You can build a flying machine, if you take your time and if you build it like a bird. I will even help you. I'll be your best friend."

22

Orville and Wilbur knew that they had made up the talking red bird, and that they were just thinking and talking to themselves. But it was fun to think of the red bird as their friend.

"Watch me!" chirped the bird. "I can fly up. I can fly down. I can turn and fly sideways. A good flying machine should be able to do everything I do."

"But lots of people have tried to build machines like birds," said Orville. "They don't work too well."

"Besides," put in Wilbur, "we don't know anything about machines. We wouldn't know where to start."

"Start at the beginning," said the bird, very sensibly. "Where else would you start? Learn about machines."

"We'll do it!" said the Wright Brothers, and they hurried off to see their father, who printed a newspaper.

"Daddy," said Wilbur, "can we help you fix the printing press when it breaks down? We want to learn about machines."

"I could surely use a couple of helpers," said Mr. Wright. "But you'll have to promise to have patience."

"What does patience mean, Daddy?" asked the Wright Brothers. Their father explained, "Patience means not getting mad when something takes a long time."

"But why do we have patience?"

"When machines break down, it can take a long time to figure out why," said Mr. Wright. "Sometimes it's hard to fix machines. If you have patience, you will keep working and not quit. Then the machine will get fixed."

"Listen to your daddy," said the bird. "He's a smart man."

One day, not long after, the printing press did break down. Orville and Wilbur tried to fix it. They tried and tried, and at first they didn't succeed.

"Oh, rats!" cried Orville at last.

"This is hard!" exclaimed Wilbur.

"Certainly it's hard," said Mr. Wright. "Lots of things are hard to do. But be patient. Don't get mad. Just keep working, and you'll be able to do almost anything you want to."

"Okay, we'll keep trying," said Orville.

"And we won't get mad," promised Wilbur.

So they kept on until they *did* fix the printing press.

"Good boys!" said their father.

As they grew up, the Wright Brothers worked on many different kinds of machines. When they were quite grown up, they opened a bicycle shop. They made bicycles and they fixed bicycles.

The chirpy little bird flew in to visit them one day.

"Now that you know so much about machines," said the bird, "when are you going to build a flying machine?"

"We're almost ready," said the Wright Brothers. "We drew up plans for the flying machine. We're going to show them to a man who knows even more about machinery than we do. We'll see what he thinks of them."

But do you know what happened when the Wright Brothers showed their plans to that man who knew all about machines?

AIR MACHINE

The man said, "It will
never fly!"

"A lot he knows!"
said the little bird.

"Be patient," sang the bird. "Don't be sad and don't get mad. Some people don't understand new ideas, and a real flying machine is a new idea.

"Besides, that man may be right. There's something wrong with the way you drew the wings. They aren't exactly like *my* wings."

"Fine, little bird, we'll keep trying," said Orville.

"And if there's something wrong with the way we've drawn the wings, you can help us," said Wilbur. "You can let us study *your* wings."

"I'd be happy to help," said the bird.

The bird's feathered friends gathered around. They were excited to see the Wright Brothers studying the bird's wings.

"When I fly," said the bird, "an area of low air pressure forms on the top side of my wings. This causes an area of high pressure on the bottom side, and the high pressure is what lifts me!

"I steer by twisting my wings a bit," the bird went on. "Look at this," said one of the Wright Brothers as he twisted a shoe box. "See, the top and bottom of it move a little. Maybe the wings on our new air machine should move, too—just like this."

"Let's study some more," said the Wright Brothers.

"And keep watching birds," said the little bird.

And so the Wright Brothers studied. They learned all they could about birds and about gliders. Gliders were like that little toy their father had brought them so long ago. They had no motors, and they could stay up in the air for a while, but not for long. They always came floating back down to the ground.

The Wright Brothers read about a man named Otto Lilienthal who was flying gliders in Germany. But he was having the same trouble everyone else was having. His gliders couldn't stay up in the air very long. They kept crashing down to the ground.

"Why don't we start by building our own glider?"
suggested Wilbur Wright.

"Perhaps if we're careful and take enough time, we
can build one that will stay up in the air for a long
time," Orville said.

So the Wright Brothers set to work carefully, not
hurrying, and they built a glider.

"I hope it will fly," said Wilbur, when they were finished.

"It may," said the bird. "The wings look pretty good. But if it doesn't fly, you mustn't get mad or discouraged. Remember, you really are *not* birds, and things can go wrong. Be patient."

41

But the Wright Brothers knew that some things
—especially the really good things—take a long time.
Sometimes you have to wait for things.

The Wright Brothers took their glider to a place called
Kitty Hawk, North Carolina, to try it out. Kitty Hawk
was a perfect place to try out a glider because there
was a lot of nice, soft sand there for the glider to land
on if it didn't stay up in the air.

They hauled the glider to the top of a little hill. Then one of the Wright Brothers climbed into the glider and the other one pushed the glider off the hill.

"It flies!" shouted the Wright Brothers.

But then, like the toy their father had given them, the glider crashed. It could fly, but not for long.

Do you know why it couldn't stay up in the air very long ?

The Wright Brothers didn't know. Neither did the little bird. "One thing I *do* know," said the bird. "This is trying even *my* patience."

"Now don't get mad, little bird. Let's remember what my father taught us," said one of the Wright Brothers. "Lots of things are hard to do, but if we keep working we can do almost anything we want to."

"We have to find a way to make the air pressure under the wings stronger," said one of the Wright Brothers. "That would lift the glider off the ground and hold it up."

"Could you put an engine in your glider?" asked the bird. "Would that do it?"

"The engine would make more wind go under the wings and keep it up in the air much longer," said one of the Wright Brothers. "It might work."

The Wright Brothers studied some more, and at last they decided they were ready. They wrote letters to people who made engines.

"We wish to purchase an engine," they wrote. "We will put the engine into a glider and make an airplane. An airplane is a glider with an engine in it."

The Wright Brothers mailed their letters, and do you know what happened?

Back came answers from the engine companies. Not one of them wanted to sell an engine to the Wright Brothers.

"I wouldn't want one of my engines to go up in anything so silly," wrote one man. "And, if people were supposed to fly, they would have been born with wings!"

What do you think the Wright Brothers did then?

They used their brains and their hands, and
they made their own engine.

It took a long, long time, but that didn't upset
the Wright Brothers. By now they knew that
everything about flying took a long time.

"At last!" said one of the Wright Brothers, when the engine was finished.

"I'm sure our engine will work," said the other.

But do you think it did?

Look at that propeller. It isn't turning. The engine wouldn't even start.

"I don't know anything about engines," said the little bird. "I only know that I learned to fly in a week or two, and it's taking you years!"

"That's O.K. We'll be patient!" said Orville.

"We won't get mad and we won't give up!" declared Wilbur. "We'll keep trying."

They did. They kept on working on their engine.

Then it happened!

The engine choked and sputtered. Then it roared loudly. The propeller spun around.

"At last! At last!" chirped the bird.

"It works!" cried the Wright Brothers.

"Now we have an engine," they said. "We'll put it into our glider. Maybe then we'll have a real airplane—one that will take off and fly."

Did they truly have an airplane?

No, they did not.

Oh, the engine worked nicely, once it was put into
the glider. But the glider couldn't fly. The engine was
too heavy.

"What will we do now?" wondered the Wright
Brothers.

"Are you going to get mad and quit?" asked the little
bird. It was quite worried.

"No, we'll work some more," sighed one of the Wright Brothers.

They went back and looked at their plans for the airplane. They made changes in the plans. They made changes in the glider. They made changes in the engine.

Then one day at Kitty Hawk a wonderful thing happened. The glider, with the engine roaring, lifted off the ground. "It flies! It finally flies!" shouted Orville. He was steering the airplane. "It's like a big bird!" It didn't fly quite as well as a bird, but it *was* the first time in the history of the world that an airplane ever lifted off the ground.

It took a long time to make an airplane fly, but when it finally happened the Wright brothers were very happy. They knew how *good* it feels when you have patience.

When you look up and see a modern airplane, you might remember how long it took to make the first airplane. You might even like to think about how you feel when you bring patience into your *own* life.

Of course, you can't invent the first airplane. That
has already been done. And what *you* may want to
do may be very different indeed! But you might like
to think about how having patience can help you.

Then perhaps you can be happier doing what you want to do . . . just like our patient friends the Wright brothers.

The End

ORVILLE WRIGHT
1871-1948

WILBUR WRIGHT
1867-1912

Wilbur Wright was born in 1867 and his brother Orville in 1871. While they lived the Wright Brothers did more than any other men to advance the art and science of aviation. They built their first glider in 1899 and flew it at Kitty Hawk, North Carolina, in 1900. The original gasoline engine was a twelve horsepower one with two propellers. The first successful flight of their heavier than air machine—their airplane—occurred on December 17, 1903, at Kitty Hawk, and it was witnessed by four men and a boy who happened to be nearby. On that day, when first they achieved powered flight, Wilbur was thirty-six and Orville thirty-two years old. The longest of those first flights was fifty-nine seconds. The Wright Brothers had a very happy Christmas that year.

Surely the value of patience was well known to the Wright Brothers. They had to try many practical changes in their designs. They had to experiment by flying in the fields and above the sand dunes. They even built a wind tunnel to discover how changes in air pressure would affect their glider or airplane. This wind tunnel was simply a gas engine hooked to a little fan which blew air through a cardboard box. They could peer through this box and see how the blowing wind affected paper wings. They patiently experimented with more than two hundred pairs of paper wings.

In 1910, the boys' father had occasion to recall the day he had brought home a little flying French toy—probably one made out of cork, wood and rubber bands. At the age of eighty-two, he had his first flight in his sons' airplane. Terribly excited, he kept crying, "Go higher! Go higher!" Few fathers have so enjoyed their sons' inventions.

In 1909, the Wright Brothers had established an aircraft manufacturing company in Dayton, Ohio, and began to turn out two airplanes a month. Before the end of his life in 1948, Orville saw planes cross every ocean and continent and fly to the North and South Poles. He even saw planes flying faster than the speed of sound.

While the Wright Brothers were eventually recognized and respected by the entire world, they were much happier when they were patiently and quietly working together. When Wilbur Wright, who lived only until 1912, was asked to make a speech at a dinner in Paris he said, "I know of only one bird—the parrot—that talks; and it doesn't fly very high."

Other Titles in the ValueTale Series